HEROES!

Draw Your Own Superheroes, Gadget Geeks & Other Do-Gooders

Jay Stephens

LARK BOOKS

A Division of Sterling Publishing Co., Inc.

New York

Library of Congress Cataloging-in-Publication Data

Stephens, Jay, 1971-
  Heroes! : draw your own superheroes, gadget geeks & other do-gooders / by
Jay Stephens. -- 1st ed.
    p. cm.
  Includes index.
  ISBN-13: 978-1-57990-934-5 (hc-plc with jacket : alk. paper)
  ISBN-10: 1-57990-934-5 (hc-plc with jacket : alk. paper)
  1. Heroes in art--Juvenile literature. 2. Cartoon characters--Juvenile
literature. 3. Cartooning--Technique--Juvenile literature. I. Title. II.
Title: Draw your own superheroes, gadget geeks & other do-gooders.
  NC1764.8.H47S74 2007
  741.5'1--dc22

                        2006101661

10 9 8 7 6 5 4 3 2 1

First Edition

Published by Lark Books, A Division of
Sterling Publishing Co., Inc.
387 Park Avenue South, New York, N.Y. 10016

© 2007, Jay Stephens

Distributed in Canada by Sterling Publishing,
c/o Canadian Manda Group, 165 Dufferin Street
Toronto, Ontario, Canada M6K 3H6

Distributed in the United Kingdom by GMC Distribution Services,
Castle Place, 166 High Street, Lewes, East Sussex, England BN7 1XU

Distributed in Australia by Capricorn Link (Australia) Pty Ltd.,
P.O. Box 704, Windsor, NSW 2756 Australia

The written instructions, photographs, designs, patterns, and projects in this volume are intended for the personal use of the reader and may be reproduced for that purpose only. Any other use, especially commercial use, is forbidden under law without written permission of the copyright holder.

Every effort has been made to ensure that all the information in this book is accurate. However, due to differing conditions, tools, and individual skills, the publisher cannot be responsible for any injuries, losses, and other damages that may result from the use of the information in this book.

If you have questions or comments about this book, please contact:
Lark Books
67 Broadway
Asheville, NC 28801
(828) 253-0467

Manufactured in China

ISBN 13: 978-1-57990-934-5 (hardcover)
ISBN 10: 1-57990-934-5 (hardcover)

For information about custom editions, special sales, and premium and corporate purchases, please contact Sterling Special Sales Department at 800-805-5489 or specialsales@sterlingpub.com.

Editor: Veronika Alice Gunter
Creative Director: Celia Naranjo
Design & Art Production: Thom Gaines
Editorial Assistance: Rose McLarney
Art Production Assistance: Robin Gregory,
    Bradley Norris
Cover Design: Jay Stephens

CONTENTS

Welcome Hero Fans! 6

HEROIC HEADS

BUFF BODIES

CRIME FIGHTER COSTUMES

COURAGEOUS COLOR

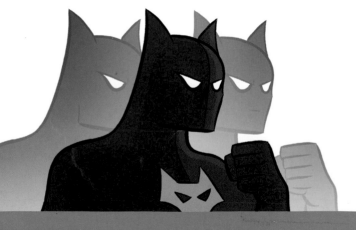

Welcome Hero Fans!

Are you hooked on heroes? Are you ready to create your own crime-crushing, villain-vanquishing champions? I'll show you how to make every kind of hero you can imagine. You may want to draw heroes like the ones you see in movies, cartoons, comic books, and on cards. Or you can invent original heroes with unheard-of powers.

Your superheroes, gadget geeks, and other do-gooders can have as much brain or brawn as you choose. They can solve any problem with mind or muscle. Your heroes might be a lot like you, with your best qualities and even your looks. And you can give them every power you ever wished for! Heroes with capes, masks, and superpowers are my favorite heroes. That explains why I've been drawing them all my life!

Every page gives you ideas for creating cool heroes. I've included a bunch of my own super characters to guide you along. The step-by-step instructions for drawing them will help you practice the skills you need to create your very own do-gooders—and the baddies they battle.

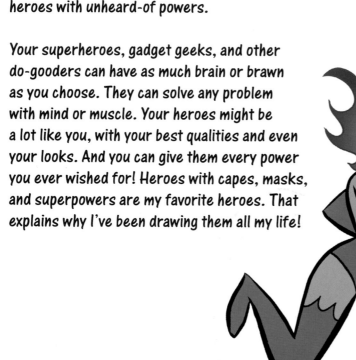

Grab a few supplies before you get started:

- Some plain, white paper (8½ x 11-inch computer paper works well)
- A regular 2H, 2HB, or 2B pencil
- A pen or fine-tipped marker (black, if possible, but dark blue will do)
- A good eraser (gum or plastic are best)
- Colored markers, pencils, or water-based paints
- OR a scanner and a computer with illustration software

Drawing is Easy

You'll use the pencil to lightly draw all sorts of marks and lines on your paper—zigzags, circles, straight lines, curved ones. (I call these construction lines.) The pen or marker is what you'll use to trace over your best hero drawings. (I call this inking the final drawing.) Then you use the eraser to get rid of the lines you aren't using. (That's why none of your marks have to be perfect—but you do need to draw them lightly so they erase easily.) There are lots of ways to add color to your final drawings. I put a whole section about it at the end of the book.

Part of learning to draw is mastering the marks you make on paper. The more you draw, the more confident you'll become. So use this book and draw a lot! But you've also got to use your head. Imagination is the most important part of making a picture. Think about what you love about heroes and who your real heroes are. Take their best qualities and make them super. Why not create a hero with more strength than a famous athlete or more smarts than your favorite teacher? Even your dog's outstanding ability to sniff out yummy sandwiches could be a superpower.

—Jay Stephens

Stories and drawings of heroes are as old as the first cave drawings. These famous faces of brave and powerful characters come from mythology and comic strips.

The ancient Icelandic god Thor wore a battle helmet and had long, flowing hair. He owned a magic hammer that would return to him after being thrown at a target. Thor had to wear special iron gloves and a super-strong belt just to pick up his hammer!

This Brainman from Mars is a typical supervillain from 1960s comic books—an ugly little guy with awesome mind-over-matter powers.

The 1941 newspaper strip <u>Miss Fury</u> introduced the first superhero created by a woman, Tarpe Mills. Miss Fury wore a costume made of black leopard skin—plus a mask with ears for a feline face!

The ancient Egyptian god Horus had the head of a falcon. Modern crime fighters often wear bat, hawk, cat, or other animal masks to conceal their identities and look more fearsome to criminals.

Of course, heroes come in all shapes and sizes... Your hero could be a baby, a noodle, or a super-flea!

© Estate of Tarpe Mills

What kind of hero will you create? Different kinds of heroes have different kinds of heads. If your super-dude is invisible, you may not even see his face!

Tough action heroes are often drawn with a big, square jaw.

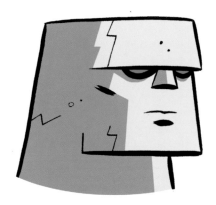

Some heroes' heads are big squares.

Using long, sharp angles will help make your bad guys look sinister.

Simple steps for sketching a head:

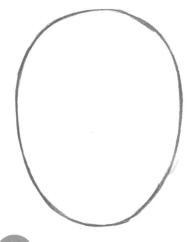

1. Use a light-colored pencil to draw an oval.

2. Draw a light cross through the middle.

Not all action heroes are rough-looking adults. Some are cute kids!

Some heroes look like monsters, even though they're do-gooders at heart.

Heroes can be beautiful. What does beautiful look like to you?

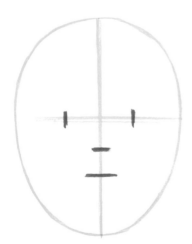

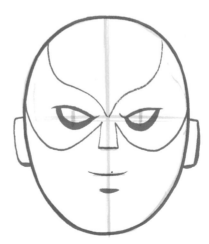

3. Make two small marks where the eyes should go, and then make two more marks for the nose and mouth.

4. Now you have a skeleton sketch to build any kind of face. Just erase the lines you don't use and trace the finished face in pencil or ink.

MASKS

Superheroes need to hide their identities.
Otherwise, people would constantly ask them to
rescue cats from trees—or show how their laser beams work.

traditional
domino mask

mask with nose

mysterious hood

solid iron!

Of course not all heroes wear masks.
The 1940s comic book champion
Crimebuster fought spies and
saboteurs in his hockey uniform! His
archenemy Ironjaw wasn't masked
either. He had a fierce metal
bear trap for a mouth.

popular cowl

full-face mask

strip mask with tie

half-head mask

this one covers
the ears

I wish you would wear a mask! UGH!

The radio and pulp magazine heroes from the 1920s and '30s like The Shadow, The Spider, and The Green Hornet used big hats, cloaks, scarves, and even theatrical make-up to disguise themselves.

This kid superhero also had an unusual sidekick—a monkey named Squeeks.

Will your hero wear a mask? What will it be? A ski mask? Scuba mask? How about a cardboard box?

(Crimebuster, Ironjaw, and Squeeks are © and ™ AC Comics.)

13

EYES

Eyes can reveal a lot about your hero: personality, emotions, or even super powers! Warhead uses his laser gaze to blast through metal and stone.

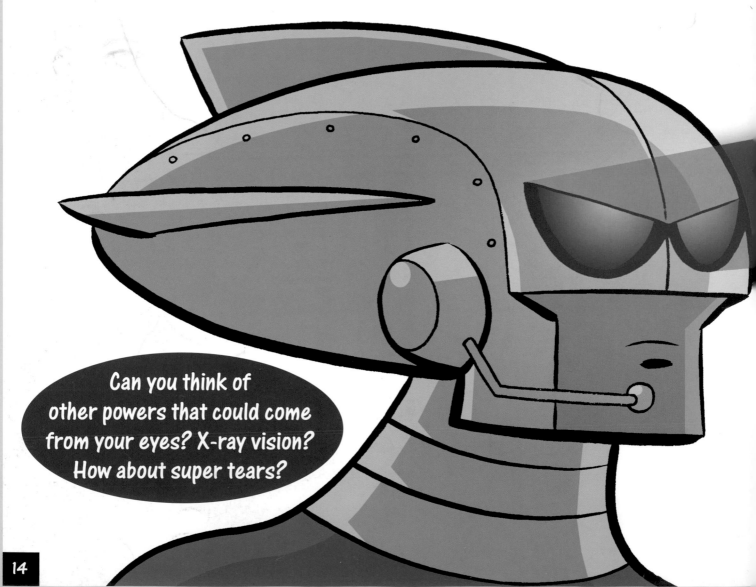

Can you think of other powers that could come from your eyes? X-ray vision? How about super tears?

A quick guide for drawing eyes:

1. Use a light-colored pencil to draw two ovals. These are the eyeballs.

2. Draw two smaller circles inside the ovals. These are the lenses. The lenses indicate where your character is looking.

3. Put two small dots inside of the smaller circles. These are the pupils.

4. Now you can add eyebrows or whatever you want!

Okay pupils, more about eyes:

Lots of heroes' eyes are blank. It gives us a look of mystery. And blank eyes are easy to draw!

Normal eyes disguise your hero as ordinary.

Big eyes look cute or young.

Arched eyebrows and dark edges look evil.

Round cartoony eyes look fun and goofy.

Sunglasses add mystery.

Night-vision goggles look high-tech.

NOSES

A nose and ears can be important crime-solving tools! Achak, P. I., relies on his keen senses to pick up clues the police might have missed.

See if you can sniff out the right nose for your action hero:

Sideways "V,"
perky and sharp

"C" shape,
jolly looking

Upside down "7,"
handsome?

Upside down "U,"
cute

Rectangular
looks tough

Number "3" shape
for a broken nose

Fat "m" shape
for shadow

How about just
the nostrils?

An elegant,
sweeping nose

"Achak" means spirit in this private investigator's native Algonquin language.

Hmmmn...Did you hear that faint scraping noise? I smell trouble! There's no time to lose!

Ears can be drawn with a simple "C" shape. (See the reverse "C" shapes below.) Drawing a sort of number "6" shape inside makes this kind of ear look more realistic.

Mutants and villains might have pointed or strangely shaped ears.

MOUTHS

Read my lips: "mouths are fun to draw." And they can transform a face! Scream Queen uses her loud mouth to stun and deafen her enemies.

Curve up for smile

Curve down for frown

Peanut shape for grimace

Sideways "7" for pout

Puckered lips are an "m" with a small curve at top and bottom

Confused or ill look

Yawn or hoot with a simple oval

A nice grin

Don't get tangled up in the details. If you can draw an "S," a zigzag, and little lines in a row, you can draw hair.

Barely there   Manga spikes   Rock 'n' Roll!

Short crewcut   Pompadour

Shoulder length

Have lots of ideas for creating your very own fantastic face yet? Think about what kind of personality you want your hero to have, and what her super skills are. Then choose the features that fit best.

There are some heads on the next few pages to get you started...

19

CREATE IT!

Practice your skills with this cybernetic crime fighter.

ONLINE

This amazing android is programmed to defend the innocent. Online is permanently connected to cyber-space and has every scrap of information the Internet has to offer at his instant disposal. But Online is more than just a smarty pants—those DigiFists hit hard in this reality, as well as the virtual one. Cyber crooks beware!

1. Draw an oval for his strong head. Two angled lines form the neck.

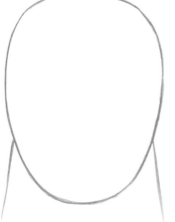

Press lightly with the pencil so you can easily erase these construction lines later.

4. Draw zigzag lines for the cheekbones. Use five straight lines to define and square-up the chin.

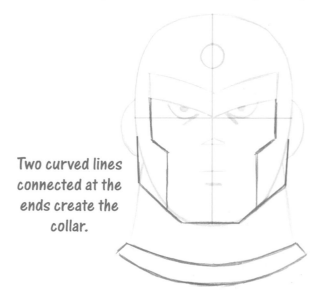

Two curved lines connected at the ends create the collar.

2. Draw two lines crossing in the middle to help you position his eyes, nose, and mouth. Create the brow with two long "V" shapes connected at the ends.

3. A circle on the forehead makes the data port (where all the information comes in). His eyes are long "U" shapes between the brow and base line.

The ear cups are "C" shapes.

The nose is a triangle.

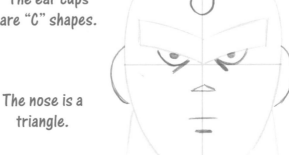

Make big dots for pupils and short lines to indicate the eye sockets.

A short line for the mouth; a shorter line for the bottom lip.

5. Use a pen or marker to trace your best construction lines.

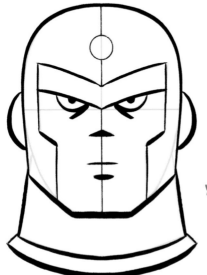

6. Time to color this hero.

A little light shadow helps define his nose.

Erase the lines you don't want to use for the final drawing.

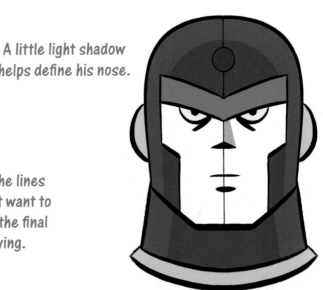

CREATE IT!

Now try a human hero—a super-human, that is.

SUPER JUICE

Keri Keener was in a one-of-a-kind juice bar accident. An electrical surge in her faulty blender bathed her in high-voltage citrus fluids—conducting a powerful mix of energy drinks. Keri woke up with yellow skin, orange hair, and a body like a battery, chock-full of electric power!

1. Begin with a squat, egg-shaped oval for her head. Two short lines create the skinny neck.

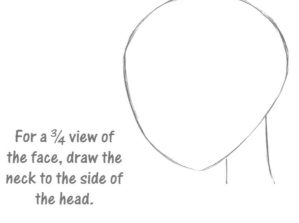

For a ¾ view of the face, draw the neck to the side of the head.

4. Draw more zigzags to make her shocking hairdo.

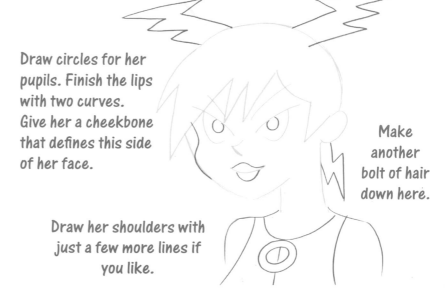

Draw circles for her pupils. Finish the lips with two curves. Give her a cheekbone that defines this side of her face.

Make another bolt of hair down here.

Draw her shoulders with just a few more lines if you like.

2. Draw four slightly curved lines to map out the eyebrows and eyelids.

3. A zigzag pattern forms her bangs. Notice where the points come down, so you can still see her face.

A backward "C" for the ear

The nose is a little slanted "L" shape.

Big curves create the eyes. A little one starts the mouth.

5. Use a pen or marker to trace your best construction lines.

Remember, you can erase all the pencil lines after you finish tracing.

6. Color her in!

Do you automatically think of a hero as big and strong? If you want to draw gigantic or muscular do-gooders, look to these classic heroes for inspiration.

According to legend, Rabbi Loew used secret Kabbalistic formulas to create the hulking Golem of Prague to protect the innocent.

A thick neck and broad shoulders make for a tough look.

Heroes don't need to be big to be tough! A Yorkshire Terrier named Smoky was a genuine World War II hero. She flew on combat missions and was awarded eight battle stars.

Jungle adventurers, like author-turned-wild girl Betty Bird from the 1940s, rely almost entirely on their well-honed physiques.

Some famous heroes are truly all muscle. American folk legend John Henry is remembered for tunneling through a mountain faster than an automatic drill—using nothing but a hammer and his bare fists!

The famous Greco-Roman hero Hercules was born mighty. He vanquished two snakes in his cot when he was only a few months old! Hercules was one of the first heroes to wear a costume. It was made from the skin of the fierce Nemean Lion.

ARMS

An arm is constructed with four parts: the shoulder, upper arm, forearm, and hand.

You can sketch out these parts as oval shapes to properly position your characters' arms.

The evil Doctor Torch blasts deadly flames from his insulated arms.

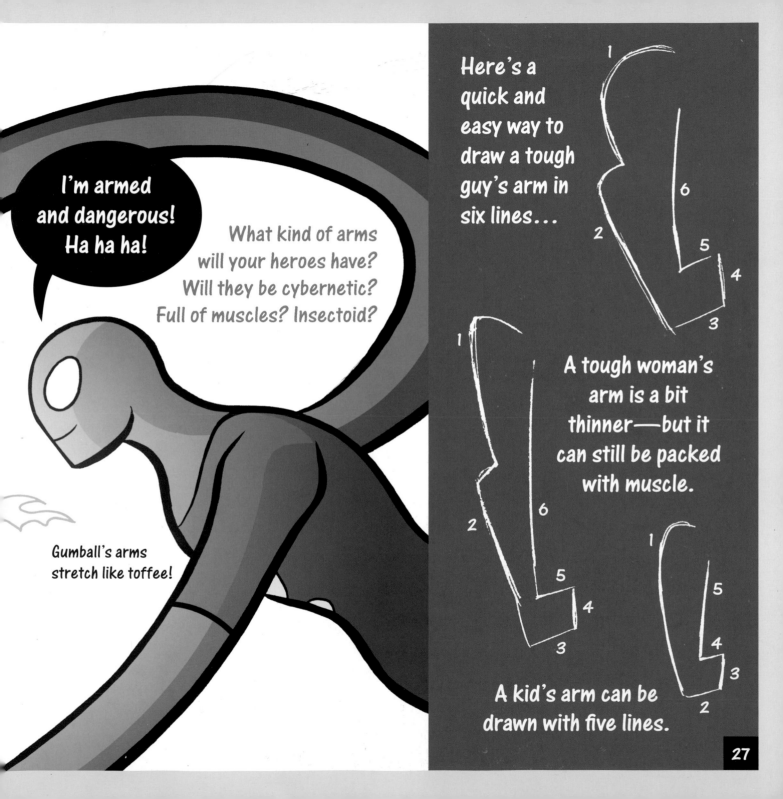

I'm armed and dangerous! Ha ha ha!

What kind of arms will your heroes have? Will they be cybernetic? Full of muscles? Insectoid?

Gumball's arms stretch like toffee!

Here's a quick and easy way to draw a tough guy's arm in six lines...

A tough woman's arm is a bit thinner—but it can still be packed with muscle.

A kid's arm can be drawn with five lines.

27

HANDS

1.

2.

3.

Sista Fista knows how powerful a hero's paws can be. Here's how to draw a hand and a fist in three easy steps.

Ow! Hey! Someone give me a hand!

WHAMMO!

Gimme five!

Knuckle sandwich!

1.

2.

3.

Some more handy tips for what your heroes might put on their mitts.

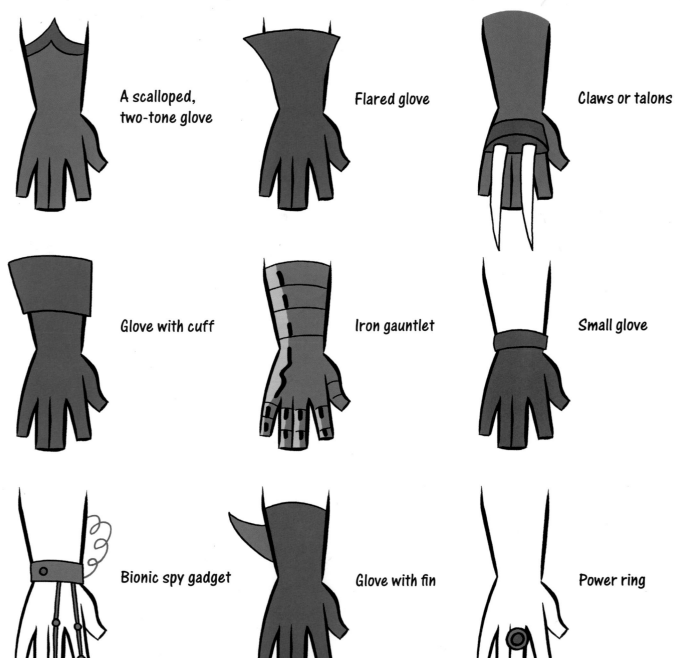

A scalloped, two-tone glove

Flared glove

Claws or talons

Glove with cuff

Iron gauntlet

Small glove

Bionic spy gadget

Glove with fin

Power ring

FEET & LEGS

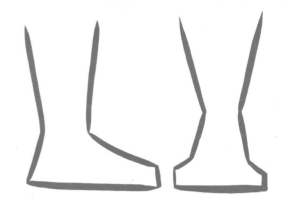

Here are a couple of ways to draw feet. Give yourself a leg up by tracing these to practice how they're constructed.

The Jiffy has really super legs! Notice how they form an "S" shape while he's running.

Will your hero run, leap, skate, or blast around town?

You can sketch a leg with four parts.
Bend them to create any leg position.

Bombface's feet are full of
fuel for blasting through things
at top speed.

Here are a few boot-iful ideas for action-hero footwear:

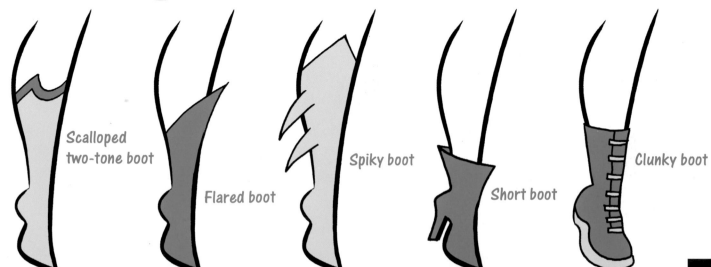

Scalloped
two-tone boot

Flared boot

Spiky boot

Short boot

Clunky boot

BODIES

Nanoman would be the first to remind you that good guys come in all shapes and sizes!

Before getting into all the details, it helps to sketch out your hero's body in light pencil.

A basic body can be made out of a large oval for the chest, two smaller ovals for the head and pelvis, and two lines for each arm and leg.

You don't have to have big muscles to fight for justice!

You can build a super-body just like you build with blocks. Angled, rectangular shapes can be used to outline your superguy or supergirl, or you can sketch a series of ovals as shown here to map out muscle.

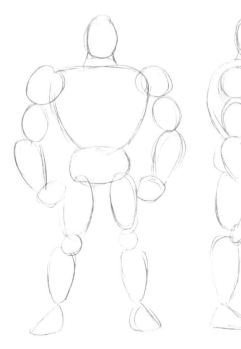

Keep your sketches light until you're ready to add the details!

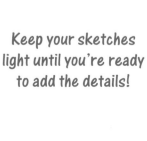

Quick-thinking heroes almost never sit still. They're always in motion— usually fighting outlaw thugs!

Here are some dynamic ideas for action poses:

A side view shows a stiff pose, almost as if Curfew is frozen in time.

When something is closer to your eye, it looks larger than the same object looks when it's farther away. This is called perspective. Try drawing your hero on a jetboard or other cool gadget that gets smaller in the distance.

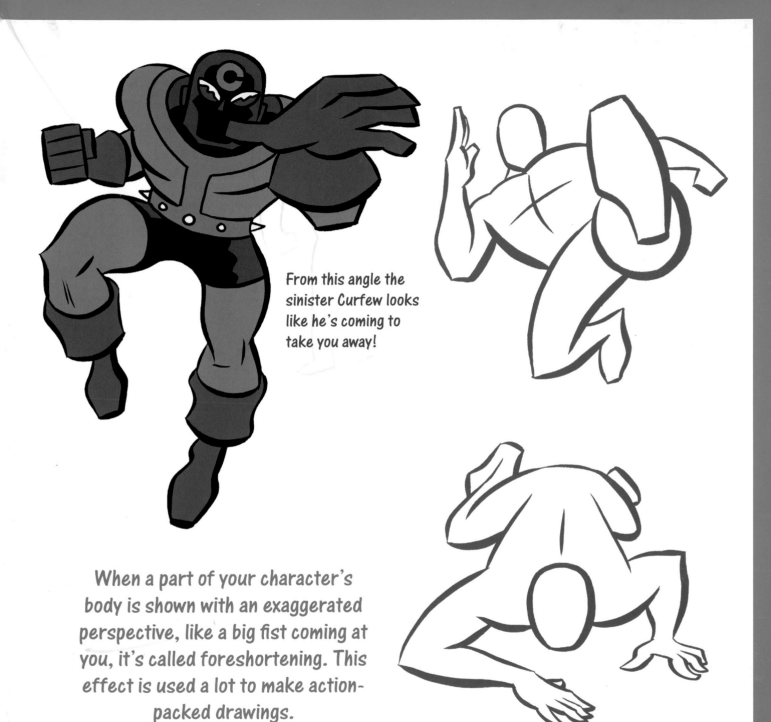

From this angle the sinister Curfew looks like he's coming to take you away!

When a part of your character's body is shown with an exaggerated perspective, like a big fist coming at you, it's called foreshortening. This effect is used a lot to make action-packed drawings.

MORE ACTION POSES

Let's try drawing a couple of action poses in three easy steps. Ready? Let's GO!!!

This pose starts off as four shapes.

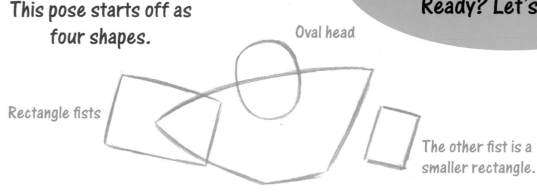

Oval head

Rectangle fists

The other fist is a smaller rectangle.

Four lines create the chest shape.

The fingers, legs, and feet are all drawn with straight lines. Only the wrists are curves.

Now you have a basic sketch to build any hero you want!

This super-heroic pose begins with the same four shapes—an oval head, rectangle fists, and a quadrilateral chest—but in different sizes and positions.

This arm is straight lines. The other one is all curved lines.

Little lines create fingers and a thumb.

The inside of the legs are straight lines. The outside lines are curved.

Are you ready to create the hero of your dreams in dynamic action! (Will he be battling baddies? Or rescuing kids from study hall?)

CREATE IT!

Meet the world's biggest, brawniest bully-buster.

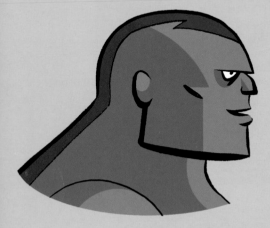

GROWTH SPURT

Nerdy Hugo Hamberg just started junior high school. Like many of his classmates, he has suddenly sprouted with the onset of adolescence. Hugo, however, has developed more than most. He can now grow at will into the massive, super-strong, do-gooder Growth Spurt. I wouldn't bully him for his lunch money if I were you!

1. A big solid guy like this starts out as six chunky blocks. Use a light-colored pencil to sketch.

Take note of how all the rectangles tilt.

This is a fist.

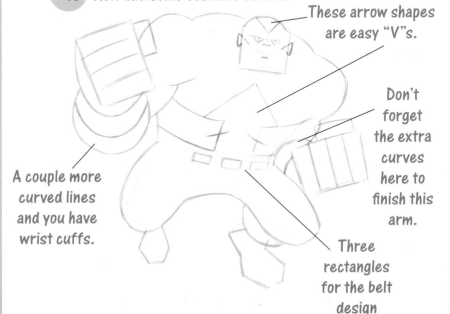

4. Now add some costume details.

These arrow shapes are easy "V"s.

Don't forget the extra curves here to finish this arm.

A couple more curved lines and you have wrist cuffs.

Three rectangles for the belt design

2. Round out the muscles with some curved lines. It looks harder to do than it is. Just copy the simple curves you see below.

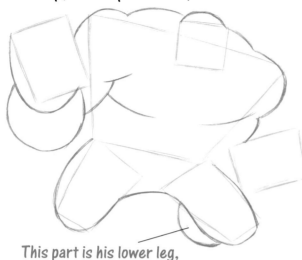

This part is his lower leg, tucked behind.

3. Make the face with a slightly "V"-shaped brow, two "V"-shaped eyes, an "M" nose, and a faint grin.

Slashes create cheekbones and define his lower lip.

Three lines make four fingers.

You can erase the construction lines as you go.

This foot is five short lines.

5. Use a pen or marker to trace your final drawing.

Only use ink over the lines you want to keep.

You can erase all of the construction lines now.

6. Color him in!

Bullies beware!

Some darker shading on part of your drawing looks dramatic and adds weight to your character.

39

CREATE IT!

This gadget-wielding action hero packs a wallop!

SISTA FISTA

Toni Thomas discovered a large metal hand in her backyard. Did it come from the explosion of a mad scientist's laboratory down the street? Toni used her brilliant mechanical mind to convert the robot fist into a versatile crime-fighting tool—much to the frustration of her insanely jealous kid brother!

1. Draw a small circle at the top with two short lines for the neck.

This weird shape is made of six lines, and is just a little bigger than the circle for the head.

Here's a long "S" zigzag. Remember to leave room for the other leg and feet.

4. Now for the details. Create Sista Fista's facial features and do-gooder gear.

Big eyes, a small backward "L" nose, and a flattened reverse "C" mouth. Some curves help define the chin and cheek.

Draw two ovals for each goggle lens. Attach them with two pairs of lines.

A few straight lines for the fingers, thumb, and glove

This triangle shape is the sap-ray.

The belt and pouch are a cinch!

2. This big, swoopy rectangle and triangle make the robot hand.

An "A" shape defines the inside of the legs.

The rest of the leg outlines are drawn with two backward "L" shapes.

3. The hair is a little tricky. Just tackle one curved line at a time.

An arm is made of two "V" shapes and a square.

Four straight lines make the fingers. Add a slight curve to make the thumb.

Draw gentle, curved lines for the boot.

Only the toe of her boot shows here.

5. Time to trace the lines you want to keep. Use a pen or marker.

You can make some of the lines a little curvier in the final drawing.

Erase the pencil construction lines.

6. Color away!

Lots of heroes rely on their brains to create great gadgets. Will your hero be one of them?

Heroes through the ages have dressed in all kinds of cool-looking clothes.

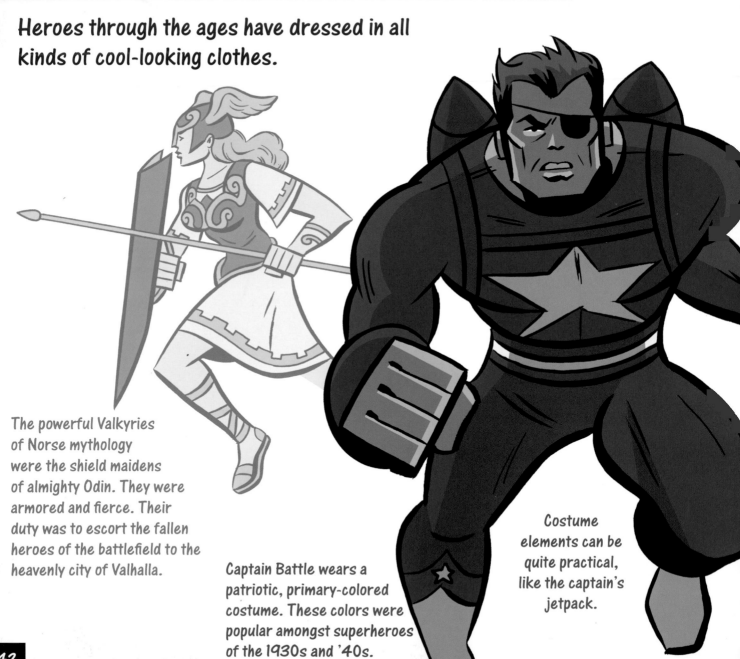

The powerful Valkyries of Norse mythology were the shield maidens of almighty Odin. They were armored and fierce. Their duty was to escort the fallen heroes of the battlefield to the heavenly city of Valhalla.

Captain Battle wears a patriotic, primary-colored costume. These colors were popular amongst superheroes of the 1930s and '40s.

Costume elements can be quite practical, like the captain's jetpack.

Some heroic characters are recognizable more for their actual physical appearance than for what they wear.

When you think Robin Hood, you think "green," right? Robin's hooded garb helped him blend into Sherwood Forest.

Famous heroes are often clad in bright colors to emphasize their purity and boldness. It also helps them stand out from bystanders and bad guys.

You can't miss the celestial Hindu god Hanuman—he's got a monkey face!

SUPER SUITS

Super suits can reflect your hero's powers and personality. An amazing outfit can even give a do-gooder special powers!

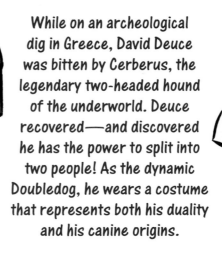

While on an archeological dig in Greece, David Deuce was bitten by Cerberus, the legendary two-headed hound of the underworld. Deuce recovered—and discovered he has the power to split into two people! As the dynamic Doubledog, he wears a costume that represents both his duality and his canine origins.

Starling's "hairplane" allows her to fly. It's her actual hair! She designed her whole costume around this most amazing feature.

Here are some other suitable ideas...

Sometimes less is more. Color can be very important.

Here's a traditional superlook.

This costume mixes some ideas together.

This bodysuit really hides your true identity!

What about a costume of pure energy?

Don't forget logos! You can create symbols, letters, or numbers that say something about your hero.

Think about who you want your character to be. Then decide what sort of costume or logo suits him or her!

ARMOR

Heroes can wear armor to protect themselves from the crooked creeps they pursue. Sometimes the armor is part of their bodies.

Whammo gets all his incredible strength from the micro-hydraulics in his battle suit. Without it, he's nothing!

Notice how this armor is built in segments like sports pads or Samurai outfits.

Will your hero wear armor? Or maybe just a goalie mask?

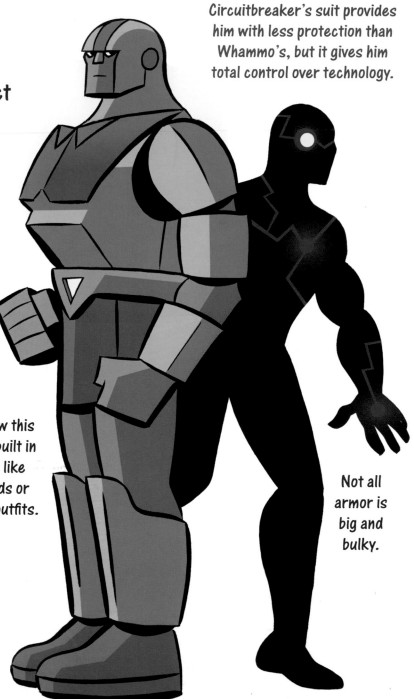

Circuitbreaker's suit provides him with less protection than Whammo's, but it gives him total control over technology.

Not all armor is big and bulky.

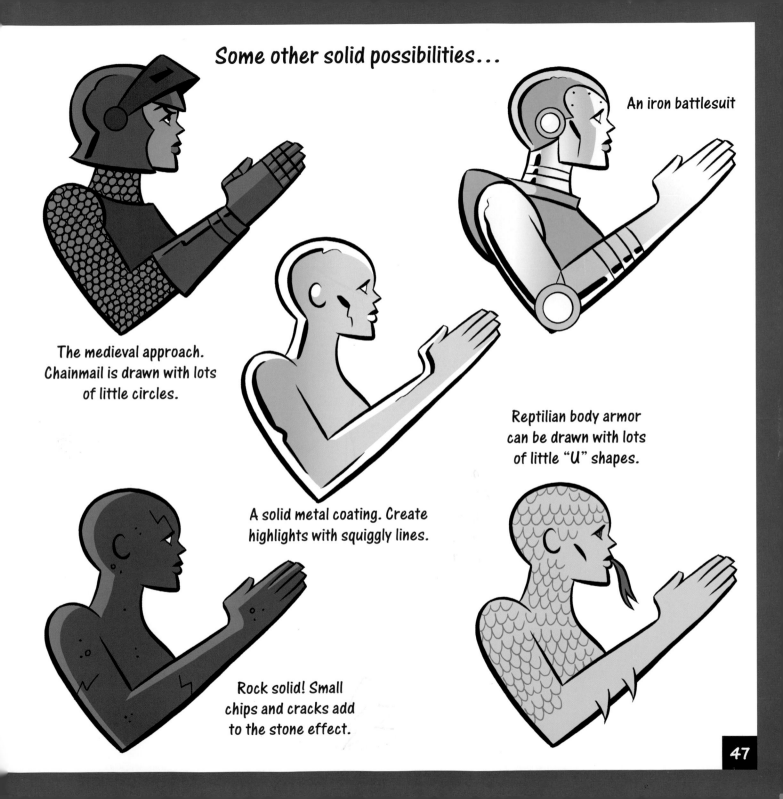

Some other solid possibilities...

The medieval approach. Chainmail is drawn with lots of little circles.

A solid metal coating. Create highlights with squiggly lines.

Rock solid! Small chips and cracks add to the stone effect.

An iron battlesuit

Reptilian body armor can be drawn with lots of little "U" shapes.

EQUIPMENT

Heroic adventurers are often equipped with wondrous weapons and high-tech gadgets. Here are some easy-to-draw ideas.

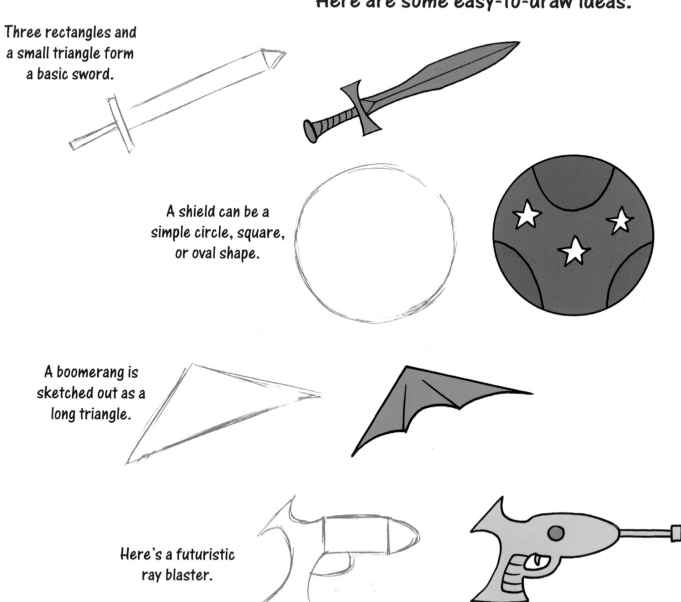

Three rectangles and a small triangle form a basic sword.

A shield can be a simple circle, square, or oval shape.

A boomerang is sketched out as a long triangle.

Here's a futuristic ray blaster.

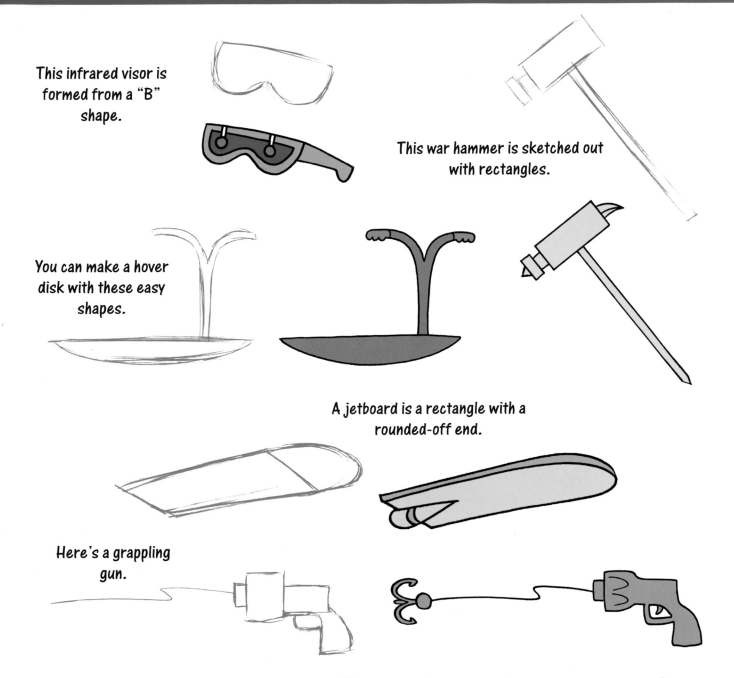

This infrared visor is formed from a "B" shape.

This war hammer is sketched out with rectangles.

You can make a hover disk with these easy shapes.

A jetboard is a rectangle with a rounded-off end.

Here's a grappling gun.

Will your hero rely on gadgets? Can you think of other cool equipment?
A wrist communicator? A mind-reading helmet?

MUTATIONS

Radiation, weird scientific experiments, and alien DNA are just a few things that can give someone super powers—and grotesque mutations!

The fearsome Subhuman can breathe both under water and on land, and has green scaly skin. Though he looks like something out of a monster movie, he's really one of the good guys.

What are you lookin' at, bub?

Will your hero look frightening? What kind of freak accident caused the mutation? Did your character accidentally inhale a radioactive dust mite?

Here are a few mutation creations...

A weird, inhuman skin color is enough to make a hero look freaky.

Horns and a tail certainly look devilish.

A furry body is a popular mutation. Keeps you warm in the winter months, too.

Maybe you'd like to go with something really odd and squiggly?

POWER EFFECTS

Superheroes like Hottie can project and control energy from within their own bodies. Does this give you a blast of inspiration for your own heroic creation?

Here are a few ideas for powerful projections...

A sonic blast of supersound

A bolt of lightning

A shower of splinters

A burst of flames

Or something unique?

To make a simple energy bolt, draw an oval where the blast begins, plus two straight lines for the path.

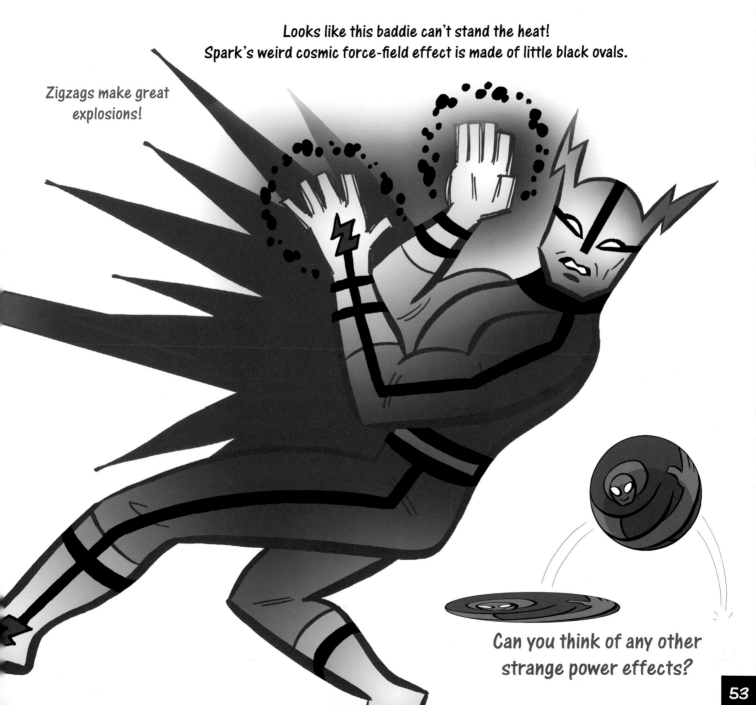

Looks like this baddie can't stand the heat!
Spark's weird cosmic force-field effect is made of little black ovals.

Zigzags make great explosions!

Can you think of any other strange power effects?

CREATE IT!

Practice drawing this mild-mannered mutant.

GUMBALL

Ray Wragley loves candy. It's not surprising that he might decide to chew a bright yellow gumball he found in the woods outside of town. After all, it looked perfectly good. It turns out the gumball was actually something from outer space. It transformed Ray into a squishy, stretchy superhero!

1. First you need to draw a slightly curved rectangle for his right hand.

Draw two big "C" shapes to create the stretchy arm.

Make a four-sided tapered shape for the chest. Leave room for the legs!

4. Just a few more parts to draw.

The eyes are egg-shaped. Don't forget the charming smile!

Short curves make the cuffs of his gloves and boots.

Draw one big circle and three smaller ones for the alien logo.

2. The head is drawn as an oval right on top of the chest shape.

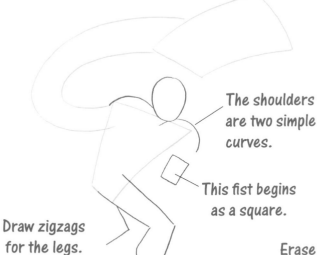

The shoulders are two simple curves.

This fist begins as a square.

Draw zigzags for the legs.

3. Finish the hand and fist with short lines for fingers.

Complete this arm with an oval and two lines.

Erase the lines you don't need anymore.

The feet are drawn with a few more little lines.

5. Trace the final drawing in pen or marker.

Erase all the pencil marks.

6. Color Gumball!

A little shading looks cool, too.

CREATE IT!

Let's try a cool effect—draw an invisible hero!

SNEAKER

When Chester Lewis found an antique bottle labeled "magic elixir," he didn't drink it like some folks might have. Instead, he poured it into his new sneakers, hoping it might improve his basketball game. It did way more than that! Chester can become invisible and move as silently as a breeze—so long as he's wearing his super shoes!

1. Draw a circle overlapping a sort of iron-shaped triangle.

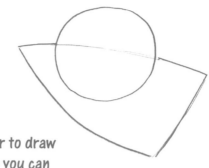

Remember to draw lightly so you can easily erase later on.

Leave room for the rest of the body.

4. Now for the details. Zigzags make the logo on Sneaker's headscarf. Draw two leaf-shaped knots at the back of his head, plus a reverse "C" ear.

The tracksuit stripes are straight lines.

Don't forget the zipper!

Add details to the shoes.
Draw these any way you like...maybe like your own shoes.

2. Add the contour of the cheek. "V" shapes make the brow and mask lines. Curves make the smile and eyes.

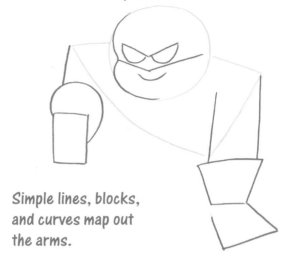

Simple lines, blocks, and curves map out the arms.

3. Draw the fingers and thumbs with little lines. The shoes can be tricky. Draw lightly and give it your best shot.

The legs are zigzags, rounded at the bottom.

Erase the construction lines you no longer need.

5. Trace over the final drawing, but instead of a dark pen or marker, use a light bluish marker. This creates the invisible effect.

6. Fill in the invisible parts with a pale blue color. If you want some parts to be visible, trace those parts with pen or marker and color them normally.

Neat, huh?

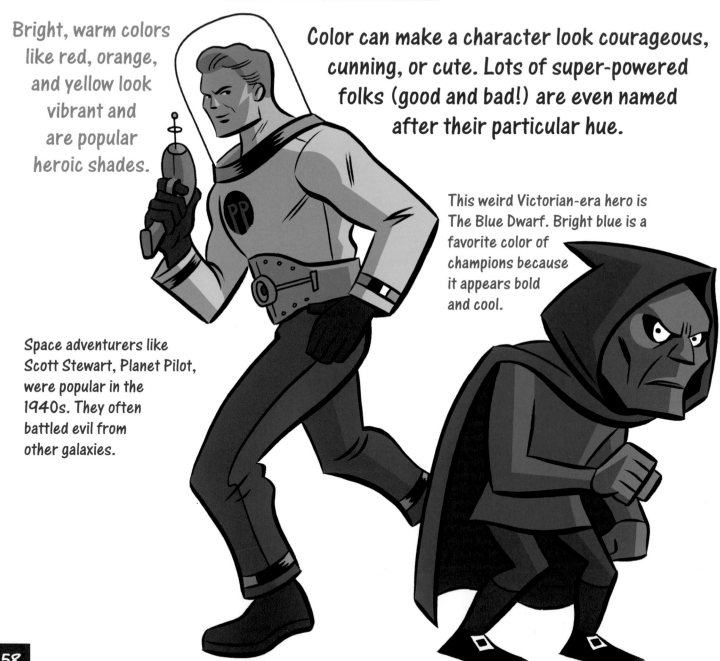

Bright, warm colors like red, orange, and yellow look vibrant and are popular heroic shades.

Color can make a character look courageous, cunning, or cute. Lots of super-powered folks (good and bad!) are even named after their particular hue.

This weird Victorian-era hero is The Blue Dwarf. Bright blue is a favorite color of champions because it appears bold and cool.

Space adventurers like Scott Stewart, Planet Pilot, were popular in the 1940s. They often battled evil from other galaxies.

Here's a primary-colored hero. Yellow, red, and blue are the purest colors in the spectrum. How does he look to you?

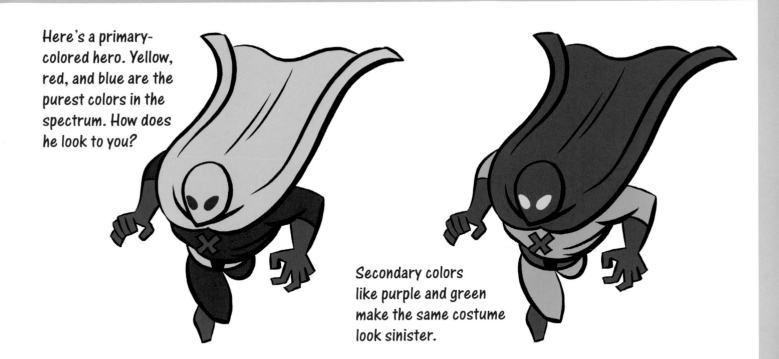

Secondary colors like purple and green make the same costume look sinister.

Generally, colder, duller tones—like pale grays, greens, blacks, and blues—make a character appear evil.

Brighter, warmer tones are supposed to inspire our confidence in a hero.

COLOR TECHNIQUES

The Green Torpedo is going to help us blast through some colorful ideas.

All of the illustrations in this book were colored on a computer.

To color yours in this way, you need to scan your finished black-and-white drawing. Then you can use an illustration program to drop in flat colors. Different programs have different ways of coloring.

Computers allow you to mix any colors you want, change colors around, and create fades and special effects. No mess to clean up, either!

Colored markers can create a similar effect.

Markers are easy to use, and provide really bold, bright colors. They're not the best for blending colors, though.

Colored pencils give you more control over blending colors and are great at creating texture.

You can get terrific shading effects from colored pencils. But they're not as good for smooth, bright color. Start with the lighter colors first if you plan to layer or blend colors.

Water-based paint can give you smooth, bold colors and the ability to blend and shade. You can water down the paint for paler tones. Just like with colored pencils, start with the lighter colors first if you plan to layer or blend colors.

Paint can be very messy, though, and it can wrinkle your paper.

HEROES!

NAME:

SECRET IDENTITY:

POWERS:

EQUIPMENT:

LIKES:

DISLIKES:

ARCHENEMY:

STORY:

By now you ought to be full of some mighty powerful ideas for creating your own cast of super characters. Maybe you also have plans for the rogues and scoundrels who are their foes! Why not start a collection of your creations? Scan, photocopy, or make your own version of the character sheet at left. Use it to record details for each of your one-of-a-kind heroes.

You can list your hero's name, secret identity, powers, and equipment. (Since every hero is different, you may come up with your own categories.) What does your hero like? (Spinach? Saving kittens from trees?) What does your hero dislike? (Flame-throwing baddies? Deep water?) There's room to include that information.

Because they're fighting for everything that's good and just in the world, do-gooders tend to make enemies. Jot down the name of your hero's archenemy—you know, that no-good evildoer who is always plotting something mean and nasty. Then write your hero's story. (How does someone become so fantastic?)

Final Word

All the instructions in this book are only ideas to get you started. They're not rules for you to follow. Use your imagination—it's one of a kind! Get started on those do-gooders. We need more heroes!

Thank Yous

Thanks to my kids, Nora and Desmond, for all their super-duper help, and to my hero, Elisabeth.

Index